CAMILLE SILVY

April 2011

To

dearest Harry

Happy Birthday

with much love

always

Peta

x

CAMILLE SILVY
PHOTOGRAPHER OF MODERN LIFE | MARK HAWORTH-BOOTH

National Portrait Gallery, London

TO ALICE MONNIER-SILVY (1839–1912)

AND FRANÇOISE MONNIER-DOMINJON

AU NOM DU DEVOIR DE MÉMOIRE

Published in Great Britain by
National Portrait Gallery Publications,
National Portrait Gallery,
St Martin's Place,
London WC2H 0HE

Published in association with the Jeu de Paume,
Paris to accompany the exhibition *Camille Silvy
1834–1910: Photographer of Modern Life* held
at the National Portrait Gallery, London, from
15 July to 24 October 2010.

For a complete catalogue of current publications,
please write to the National Portrait Gallery
at the address above, or visit our website at
www.npg.org.uk/publications

ISBN: 978 185514 415 6

A catalogue record for this book is available
from the British Library.

10 9 8 7 6 5 4 3 2 1

Head of Publications: Celia Joicey
Managing Editor: Christopher Tinker
Editor: Claudia Bloch
Production: Geoff Barlow and Ruth Müller-Wirth
Design: Studio Dempsey

Front cover *Studies on Light: Twilight*,
1859 (detail), see Plate 33

Frontispiece *Studies on Light: Fog*,
1859 (detail), see Plate 31

Back cover *The Misses Marjoribanks*,
1861, see Plate 83

Contents

Foreword

*Modernity is the transient, the fleeting, the contingent; it is
one half of art, the other being the eternal and the immutable.*
CHARLES BAUDELAIRE, 1863

The increasing complexity and intensity of city life in the nineteenth
century produced a desire in artists and writers to portray their
changing surroundings vividly and directly. Artists who flourished
in Paris at this time were less concerned with grand historical or
allegorical themes and were determined to convey the experience of
their own lives and those around them. As photography emerged from
its predominantly experimental beginnings to become artistically
and commercially engaged, those photographic artists who could take
the processes beyond the documentary or scientific began to create
wonderful images of this new era.

Camille Silvy (1834–1910), who worked in both France and Britain, is
an under-recognised star of this startlingly fresh wave of photography.
The soft light of his *River Scene* was understandably appealing to
those who were encased in the bustle and smoke of the metropolis.
And his touch here is as sure as when he positioned his subjects, with
sympathetic props and backdrops, for a brand-new carte-de-visite
portrait. Many of the visitors to his fashionable London studio would
have found the experience of being photographed strange, but the
results form an exquisite and special cache of individual likenesses.

A hundred years after his death and following extensive research by
Mark Haworth-Booth and other photographic scholars, this is the first
occasion on which Silvy's work can be appropriately appraised. Our first
thanks therefore go to Mark Haworth-Booth, as both originator and
curator of the *Camille Silvy: Photographer of Modern Life* exhibition
and as the perceptive author of this book. His long experience as an
expert in photographs has been brought to bear on an artist who
already holds a special place in the photographic collections of the

National Portrait Gallery. He has collaborated with colleagues at the Jeu de Paume in Paris: Veronique Dabin, Head of Exhibitions Department, Judith Czernichow, Exhibitions Coordinator, Elisabeth Galloy, Coordinator Travelling Exhibitions and Françoise Bonnefoy, Head of Publications and with those at the National Portrait Gallery in London: Peter Funnell, Curator of 19th Century Portraits, Terence Pepper, Curator of Photographs, Constantia Nicolaides, Photographs Cataloguer, Sarah Tinsley, Head of Exhibitions, Sophie Clark, Exhibitions Manager, Celia Joicey, Head of Publications, and Claudia Bloch, Editor. We are grateful for their many creative and logistical contributions.

We should also like to thank staff at the National Portrait Gallery, including Pim Baxter, Sara Bunting, Naomi Conway, Andrea Easey, Ian Gardner, Michelle Greaves, Justine McLisky, Eleanor Macnair, Ruth Müller-Wirth, Doris Pearce, Jonathan Rowbotham, Jude Simmons, Liz Smith, Christopher Tinker, Helen Whiteoak and Ulrike Wachsmann.

Final and special thanks are due to the lenders to the exhibition, both public and private collections, to Alice Monnier-Silvy's family and especially to Françoise Monnier-Dominjon for her insight, enthusiasm and assistance with the project.

Marta Gili
Director, Jeu de Paume, Paris

Sandy Nairne
Director, National Portrait Gallery, London

Preface

Camille Silvy (1834–1910) was one of the stars of the second wave of pioneer photographers. The first wave included the rival inventors of photography, William Henry Fox Talbot (1800–77) and Louis-Jacques-Mandé Daguerre (1787–1851), who announced the new medium to the world in 1839. If the 1840s represented an age of photographic experimentation and the first miraculous but often stiff and sometimes cadaverous-looking portraits, the 1850s saw broader professionalisation and an increasingly natural-looking portraiture. A key date was 1855, when a great World's Fair in Paris showed off photography to large new audiences. Among the highlights were photographs of actors and actresses. Suddenly, fans could see authentic, close-up pictures of their heroes and heroines. Silvy was then twenty-one years old. Although he was working for the French diplomatic service, two years later he took up photography and the following year emerged as a major talent. In 1859 he moved from Paris to London and opened a portrait studio. It soon became the talk of the town. Silvy rode the crest of a new craze, which began in Paris that year, swept over the English Channel and sped across the Atlantic.

The new fashion was for albums of carte-de-visite (visiting card) portrait photographs. The best description was published in a topical magazine article when the fad was at its height in 1862:

> Those albums are fast taking the place and doing the work of the long-cherished [visiting] card-basket. That institution has had a long swing of it. It was a good thing to leave on the table that your morning-caller while waiting in the drawing-room till you were presentable, might see what distinguished company you kept, and what very unexceptionable people were in the habit of coming to call on you. But the card-basket was not comparable to the album as an advertisement of your claims to gentility. The card of Mrs Brown of Peckham would well to the surface at times from the depths to which you had consigned it, and overlay that of your favourite countess or millionaire. Besides, you could not

in so many words call attention to your card-basket as you can to your album. You place it in your friend's hands, saying, 'This only contains my special favourites, mind,' and there is her ladyship staring them in the face the next moment. 'Who is this sweet person?' says the visitor. 'Oh, that is dear Lady Puddicombe,' you reply carelessly. Delicious moment![1]

Silvy, who featured in the article as the carte-de-visite photographer par excellence, already had – another author pointed out – 'the negatives of sitters in number equal to the inhabitants of a large country town …'. Although his sittings were expensive and therefore exclusive to the wealthy classes, the resulting portraits – because of their low unit cost – retailed at modest prices. Silvy made his studio into a portrait factory and distributed his photographs by the hundreds of thousands through the firm of Marion & Co. at 152 Regent Street in central London. This amazing emporium was

by far the largest dealer in *cartes de visite* in the country; indeed, they do as much as all the houses put together. The wholesale department of this establishment, devoted to these portraits, is in itself a sight. To this centre flow all the photographs in the country that 'will run'. Packed in the drawers and on the shelves are the representatives of thousands of Englishwomen and Englishmen awaiting to be shuffled out to all the leading shops in the country.[2]

Collecting these representative 'Englishwomen and Englishmen' into albums offered ways – as we would say nowadays – of constructing and exploring social identities. They were the social networking site of their time.[3]

Silvy was a 'modern' in many ways. He was, as this book will reveal, the first photographer to write about the division between 'personal' and 'commercial' work. In some ways, Silvy's career prefigures that of the American photographer Irving Penn (1917–2009). Penn held a place

at the top of New York's fashion, portrait and commercial photographic scene for over sixty years — but constantly found time to pursue his own private projects in photography. Just as Penn made experimental works, including the astonishing self-portraits of the 1980s and 1990s, so, as we shall see, did Silvy — more than a century earlier, when fashion and portrait photography were young.[4]

Unlike Penn, Silvy enjoyed only a brief career in photography — a mere ten years — from 1857 to 1867. He passed like a comet over Second Empire Paris and High Victorian London, bequeathing us one of the most original oeuvres in the whole history of photography. After his death, Silvy was remembered in key books and exhibitions. In 1939 he was prominently included in an exhibition held at the Victoria and Albert Museum (V&A) that celebrated the first 100 years of photography. Silvy featured in the first paperback history of photography published in the same year.[5] He was given enthusiastic, if not always accurate, attention in landmark publications such as Helmut and Alison Gernsheim's *History of Photography* (1955) and Cecil Beaton's *The Magic Image* (1975). He also appeared in key exhibitions such as the V&A's *From Today Painting is Dead* (1972) and the Royal Academy's *The Art of Photography, 1839–1989* (1989). Since then, the experts whose works appear in the bibliography have more fully illuminated Silvy, his period and the carte-de-visite phenomenon. However, since the time of Silvy's retirement from photography in 1868, much of his most extraordinary work was preserved, unknown to scholars, in a private collection in Paris. It is only now, in 2010 — the centenary of his death — that we can at last bring together the cream of Silvy's achievement and understand its true significance for the first time.

Mark Haworth-Booth

Adelina Patti
as Harriet in *Martha*,
1861
see Plate 40

For notes see page 152

Chapter 1 | Introducing Camille Silvy

Chapter 1 | Introducing Camille Silvy

Camille Silvy is one of the great French photographers of the nineteenth century. Silvy photographed in a ten-year creative burst from 1857 to 1867, which placed his career at the heart of the surge of economic, technological, industrial and cultural change that produced the modern world. A self-portrait from 1863 shows Silvy repeated again and again, like an image from Andy Warhol's studio (Plate 1). Silvy photographed landscapes, twilight, fog, city streets and how people wore fashionable dress. He came closest in photography to embodying the vision of 'the painter of modern life' sketched out by Charles Baudelaire (1821–67) in his famous essay of the same title.[1] The photographer Nadar (1820–1910) remembered Silvy as one of the 'Primitives' of photography – the enthusiasts who first embraced and defined the medium.[2] Another distinguished photographer, Thomas Sutton (1819–75), called Silvy a 'photographic genius'.[3] Silvy pioneered many now familiar branches of the medium, transformed it from an art into an industry, and created some of the most beautiful photographs of all time.

Silvy made elegant portraits of extraordinary people. He showed us a London that was far more cosmopolitan, and ethnically diverse, than we might have imagined. Equally important is the way Silvy portrayed uncelebrated people – the professional or business men and the country gentry, their wives, children and sometimes their servants. They and Silvy pioneered the modernisation – and, in the end, democratisation – of portraiture.

In 1992 I wrote *Camille Silvy: River Scene, France* (Plate 2), the first book on Silvy. His descendants in Paris generously aided my research – as they have done for the past twenty years. They provided authentic data about Silvy – the accounts of him in print up to that time had been somewhat fanciful. Thanks to newly discovered documents, today we can trace Silvy's career in even more vivid detail.[4]

Camille-Léon-Louis Silvy was born on 18 May 1834 in the market town of Nogent-le-Rotrou in the Eure-et-Loir *département*, about an hour's drive west of Chartres. Silvy's father, Onésipe, was

Plate 2

La Vallée de l'Huisne
(River Scene, France), 1858
305 x 420mm

Plate 3

Reproduction from a
photographic portrait of
Camille Silvy (*c*.1853),
c.1862
105 x 112mm

mayor of the town from 1832 to 1835 and Marie-Louise, his mother, was the daughter of a doctor from a local land-owning family. Silvy's father was also a lawyer and later a director of a Paris bank, the Caisse Hypothécaire. Silvy himself graduated in law at the age of eighteen and took up a diplomatic post in the French foreign office in 1853. The earliest photographic portrait of Silvy probably dates from this time (Plate 3). Nadar recalled Silvy's 'youthful, michelangelesque features, the thoroughly academic correctness of his figure, and that classical purity of gesture that gives grace and rhythm to every gesture.'[5] He was posted to London the following year. Judging from a scrap album he kept, Silvy could have become a fashionable young man about town, a soldier or – like Constantin Guys (1802?–92), Baudelaire's model 'painter of modern life' – a magazine illustrator.[6] A watercolour in Silvy's scrap album shows a ruddy-faced Englishman, perhaps a coach driver, holding a foaming pewter mug outside a pub. A skinny man beside him, wearing tight-fitting grey leggings and a tartan waistcoat, reads aloud from a broadsheet newspaper (Plate 4). Silvy was to merge photography with illustration and, to achieve this, he pioneered some audacious manipulations that anticipate the digital age.

While in London in 1854, Silvy got to know the photographer Leonida Caldesi (1823–91). His portrait of Silvy in the scrap album was an early exercise in a new photographic technology – the wet collodion process, which had been invented in England in 1851 and taken up universally over the next few years. The process was laborious because the glass negative had to be coated with a solution of silver salts on site and developed immediately after exposure. However, the benefits were speed and greatly enhanced sharpness. Silvy was soon to use these new techniques to the full.

Chapter 2 | Early photographs:
Algeria and rural France

Chapter 2 | Early photographs: Algeria and rural France

While still a diplomat, Silvy visited Algeria in 1857 on a commission from the Minister of Public Instruction to draw buildings and scenes, as France was eager to encourage emigration to its new colony. Silvy travelled with his former drawing master, François Hippolyte Lalaisse (1812–84). However, 'when I realised the inadequacy of my talent in obtaining exact views of the places we travelled through, I dedicated myself to photography and … concentrated especially on reproducing everything interesting, archaeologically or historically – that presented itself to me.'[1] Silvy made accomplished photographs and one that was exceptional – a view of the second floor gallery of a Moresque villa in Algiers, a recumbent man smoking a pipe of hashish among the shadows (Plate 5). The tenebrous setting evokes a hallucinogenic waking-dream.[2]

On his return to France, Silvy studied with a highly original amateur photographer, Count Olympe Aguado (1827–94). The Silvys had acquired Gaillard, a farmhouse some eighteen kilometres east of Nogent in the hamlet of La Croix-du-Perche, and it was here that Silvy photographed the millpond, a ford (Plate 6), a cider press (Plate 7) and livestock (Plate 8). In 1858 Silvy made two photographs of *trophées de chasse* (hunting trophies) hanging on a barn door on which he chalked 'Gaillard', his initials and the date. One photograph shows the barrel of a gun projecting from the top margin of the print in a bold piece of illusionism (Plate 9).

Silvy made an attempt at photographing the River Huisne in Nogent-le-Rotrou from across the meadow (Plate 10), which is still there today. For his most famous work, *River Scene, France* (Plate 2), Silvy placed his camera on a bridge over the river. On the left he positioned a young man and a young woman, apparently about to set off on a boating trip. On the right he posed a group of working people. Broader access to leisure, a by-product of the systematic reorganisation of work, was new in the 1850s – the decade when London invented the music hall, Paris the Bois de Boulogne and New York its Central Park.[3]

Plate 6

The ford at
La Croix-du-Perche,
c.1858
246 x 185mm

Plate 7

The cider press at
La Croix-du-Perche,
c.1858
235 x 181mm

The wet collodion process was overly responsive to the blue part of the colour spectrum and so it was almost impossible to combine ground and sky on one negative. The solutions were to black out the sky on a landscape negative so it would print white (as in Plate 10); to 'shade' it to suggest tone; to paint in clouds on the negative; or to print in a sky from another negative (as Silvy did in Plate 2). Silvy's early masterpiece was exhibited and acclaimed in Edinburgh and London before being shown in Paris in spring 1859, as *La Vallée de l'Huisne*. It appeared in a group of twenty works by Silvy in the first ever Salon of photography as a fine art, held in the Palais de l'Industrie in the Champs Elysées, alongside the Salon des Beaux Arts. Critics picked out Silvy as a rising star.[4]

A fascinating version of the photograph was discovered by the photography expert Marc Pagneux in 2004, which had been printed by Silvy in 1859. When he gave it to his lawyer, a Monsieur Beaurepaire, in Saumur on 7 May 1875, Silvy added annotations (Plate 11). He confirmed that the landscape was composed from two wet collodion glass negatives. One of them has breakages in the two top corners; the top edge of the other negative can be seen (unbroken) above those breaks. Silvy tells us that he used a simple triple lens made by Lerebours et Secretan in Paris. The exposure time for each negative was three to four seconds. The group on the right bank were *'Employé du Ch[em] in de fer'* (railway workers). Silvy named the *'opérateur'* (the camera operator) as Félix Moutarde, who focused the camera beautifully except that he inadvertently included the edge of the bridge at the base and part of either himself or the portable dark tent on the left. These errors, together with the breakages at the top, show why Silvy cropped his landscape to an oval and burned-in the foreground.

Another version of the *River Scene, France* appeared four years later (Plate 12). Silvy gave it to Aristide Gouverneur, a printer and publisher in Nogent, in recognition of his new edition of the Pléiade poet, Remy Belleau (1528–77). Silvy inscribed lines from Belleau's 'Ode à Nogent' on the mount. Comparison of

the three versions (Plates 2, 10 and 11)
show that the foreground is different in
each case. Silvy drew a line of cloud on
the negative just above the horizon at
the right and created some cypress-like
trees at the centre of the composition,
omitting a trunk for one of them (see the
detail of Plate 2, p.31). His intention was
to make the viewer read the composite
halves of the picture as one. Silvy was
already a master illusionist.

Plate 8

Study of sheep, *c.*1858
127 x 160mm

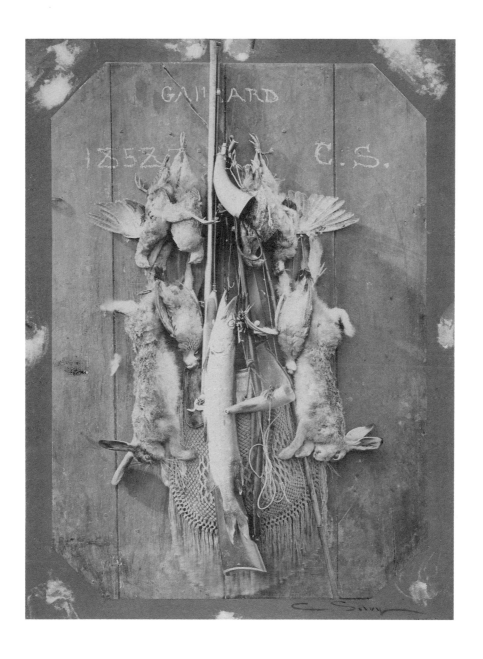

Plate 9

Trophées de chasse
(Hunting trophies), 1858
244 x 162mm

Camille Silvy

Plate 10

View of Nogent-le-Rotrou,
Eure-et-Loir, from the
meadows, *c*.1858
290 x 395mm

Camille Silvy

Plate 12

River Scene, France,
inscribed with lines
by Remy Belleau, 1858
(printed 1859)
258 x 552mm

Chapter 3 | 1859: Silvy moves
from Paris to London

Chapter 3 | 1859: Silvy moves from Paris to London

Napoleon III (1808–73), Emperor of the French 1852–70, sent an army to Italy to drive out the Austrians in 1859. The Emperor reached Genoa on 12 May and drafted an *Ordre du Jour* (Order of the Day) to the army. The text was sent to Paris by electric telegraph, printed overnight and posted in the streets at dawn. This was intended to demonstrate that, although the Emperor was away, he was still in control. Baudelaire remarked: 'the supreme glory of Napoleon III, in the eyes of History and of the French People, will have been to prove that anybody can govern a great nation as soon as they have got control of the telegraph and the national press.'[1] Silvy restaged and photographed the scene (as shown in Plate 13). Copies of his photograph were sold by Goupil & Co., admired at court and published as a wood-engraving in the magazine *L'Illustration*.[2]

The photographer A.A.E. Disdéri (1819–89), who once worked in a lithographer's atelier, invented the technique of exposing small portrait photographs in multiples of six or eight on one negative. This meant that the sitter could be photographed in different poses, which would then be printed on one sheet. There are many connections between lithography and cartes-de-visite; however, the relationship may be even more direct than hitherto proposed.[3] Disdéri would have been familiar with sheets of repeated illustrations like the one from 1853 reproduced in Plate 14. This is probably an uncut sheet of commercial visiting cards. Here, I believe, is the model Disdéri adapted when he patented the photographic carte-de-visite the following year; and within five years cartes had become a Paris fad. Silvy played a major role in introducing the format to London and making it a craze. Photography learned a mass-production technique from an older technology (Plate 15). Lithographic workshops are also likely to have provided the model for new photographic studios organised on an industrial scale.

In the summer of 1859 Silvy gave up his diplomatic career and moved to London. He took over the photographic studio of Caldesi and Montecchi at 38 Porchester Terrace in Bayswater,

Camille Silvy

Plate 14 (Below)

Uncut proof sheet of
visiting cards for Kohlsaat
Brothers, New York
Printed by J. Lemercier &
Cie, Paris , 1854
Each image: 90 x 56mm
Sheet: 280 x 394mm

Plate 15 (Right)

Proof sheet of Madame
Silvy, c.1865
223 x 290mm

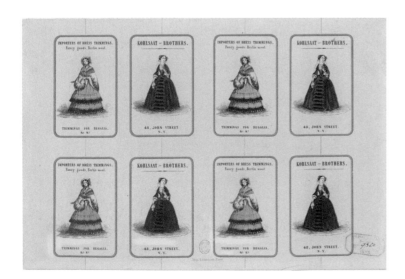

Plate 16

View of the house –
entrance to Silvy studio,
38 Porchester Terrace,
*c.*1862
86 x 70mm

Plate 17

Self-portrait, Silvy in the
studio, *c.*1859
225 x 188mm

then being developed on the north side of Hyde Park. The house (Plate 16) had been built in 1829–30 for the painter John Linnell (1792–1882). Silvy photographed himself in the studio, with its glazed roof, blinds to control the light, a tapestry embroidered with a coat of arms and a sculpture of a falconer (Plate 17). The glass-room for portraiture is at the right. In one portrait Silvy used a camera as an accessory (Plate 18). It had two lenses: an exposure would be made using one lens, the negative would then be moved into a different position and the second lens used for a new exposure on a different section of the same plate. Each lens could record three images on the negative.[4] Some Silvy proof portraits have survived with crosses indicating the sitter's choice (Plate 19). Surviving untrimmed cartes show how the glass-room was set up, with oblique top-lighting, as well as a large window at the side (Plate 20). There was a pelmet, behind which a painted backdrop was positioned, and from which drapery was suspended. The pelmet reduced the light on the backdrop so that the figure stood out against it. At the left was a reflecting screen covered in white paper

or calico, which bounced light back onto the sitter. In her Ph.D. thesis on Victorian portrait photography, Juliet Hacking has convincingly suggested that in the morning Silvy's sitters were lit from the right and in the afternoon from the left.[5]

Nadar remembered Silvy as a 'formally clad, white-tied charmer who – as each client entered the studio – would negligently cast a pair of white gloves into an already overflowing basket, and don another, irreproachably new pair …'.[6] The charm is evident in the early portrait of the Honourable Mrs Carnegie, whose reflection displayed her unexpected décolleté and lovely smile. Gloves were presumably required because Silvy would physically arrange his clients, however noble (Plate 21). The young duc de Penthièvre balances his weight on one foot, rests a hand on the balustrade beside him and tilts his head to the left (Plate 22). Daylight from the upper right accentuates the brow. There is no evidence that Silvy resorted to a posing-stand and the effect is simple, natural and nonchalant. The exposures were very short – almost instantaneous.[7] Dresses needed careful arrangement

Plate 18

Charles Henry Tamworth
Hanbury-Tracy, 1866
82 x 55mm

Plate 19

Marked proof sheet of
Lady Grey de Wilton,
1860
115 x 176mm

Plate 20

Lord Saye of Sale, proof
sheet detail, 1860
210 x 260mm

by a female assistant and perhaps
'Mlle Marie', as she is identified in
the Daybooks, was such a helper (see
Plate 24). The elegant contrapposto of
a young woman (Plate 23) was enabled
by a deftly positioned footstool, one
shining foot of which can be glimpsed
under the crinoline on the left. Silvy
photographed his studio dressing-room
(Plate 25). A photography manual
from 1854 recommended that studios
should include 'an appropriate room,
with female attendant [which] admits
of the lady's toilet, so that an evening
dress, fancy or other costume can be
conveniently adopted.'[8]

Rotten Row in Hyde Park was London's
major space for fashionable display on
horseback. Silvy, an expert horseman,
photographed another aspect of the
equestrian scene, horseshoeing in
Buckingham Palace Road (Plate
26). The multiple ingredients of this
photograph combine to give a complex
city picture. Silvy made an equestrian
portrait of Viscount Sydney in the yard
behind the studio. This is the first
photograph in Volume 1 of the twelve
Daybooks of C. Silvy & Co. preserved

by the National Portrait Gallery (Plate
27). The Viscount was Queen Victoria's
Lord Chamberlain, and thus head of
the royal household, from 1859 to 1866.
The Viscount was followed, in the first
Daybook alone, as Juliet Hacking has
pointed out, by '3 Dukes, 8 Duchesses,
3 Counts, 23 Countesses, 3 Marquises,
8 Marchionesses, 10 Viscounts, 8
Viscountesses, 32 Lords and 110 Ladies'.
Hacking's research suggests that women
commissioned more portraits than men
by a ratio of around two to one.[9] Silvy
wrote to his father on 8 June 1860 that
'The Queen continues to send me all
the people in her household, the first
portraits that I made of them being
very much appreciated.'[10]

In a letter to his father on 22 August
1859, Silvy noted that the standard
of English portrait photography was
technically low, as were the prices.
While Leonida Caldesi charged thirty
shillings for a sitting, Silvy charged
double – three guineas, with half a
guinea for each extra print supplied.
These prices would have been for larger
portraits rather than for the cartes.
Silvy charged two guineas for a sitting

Plate 21

Louisa Albertina
Carnegie (née Hope), 1860
86 x 55mm

Plate 22

Pierre d'Orléans, duc de
Penthièvre, 1860
81 x 56mm

Plate 23

Miss Helen Bagge, 1861
104 x 84mm

Plate 24

Mlle Marie, 1860
86 x 57mm

Plate 25

Clients' dressing room,
c.1860
106 x 82mm

for forty carte-de-visite portraits and clients could order additional cartes by the dozen. Celebrity cartes were available at 1/6d., and twice that if hand-coloured.[11] Soon afterwards he photographed Lady Otway executing a piaffe, in which the horse simultaneously raises a foreleg and a back leg (Plate 28). He not only updated the tradition of equestrian painting (as can be seen in Plate 29), but also photographed the sleek carriages and smart grooms recommended by Baudelaire to his painter of modern life (Plate 30).[12]

Silvy wrote to his father on 5 December 1859 with understandable excitement. The previous Saturday, his inventor neighbour, Monsieur Joubert, had taken Silvy's studies of *Fog, Sun* and *Twilight* to Windsor Castle (Plates 31–33). Queen Victoria (1819–1901) and Prince Albert (1819–61) had greatly admired them, especially *Twilight*. Silvy went on to tell his father about a magazine in which he would publish his photographs that would appear monthly and by the end of the year comprise a very beautiful album. Silvy envisaged a page of

Plate 26

J. Yaxley Veterinary Forge, Buckingham Palace Road, London, *c.*1860
224 x 251mm

Plate 27

Viscount Sydney, 1859
92 x 78mm

Plate 28

Eliza Price (née Noble),
Lady Otway, 1860
81 x 60mm

Plate 29

Lad and horses, *c.*1860
130 x 135mm

Plate 30

Lady in a carriage drawn
by two black horses,
groom in attendance,
c.1860
110 x 150mm

Plate 31

Studies on Light: Fog,
1859
275 x 220mm

text accompanying his photographs and, in order to raise the necessary subscriptions, he intended to ask the writer Charles Dickens (1812–70) to lend his name to the enterprise. *Bleak House* (1852–3), with its fog, gas-lamps, and crossing-sweeper, seems to inform Silvy's London street photographs.

The *London Photographic Review* was first published, without any involvement by Dickens, in January 1860. The contents of the first issue were described as one photograph entitled *Evening Star*, plus – for those taking out a year's subscription – 'two additional photographs which, with Part I, "Evening Star", will form one of the Series of the Studies on Light by C. Silvy'. He titled the photographs as follows:

BROUILLARD – SOLEIL – CREPUSCULE
FOG – SUN – TWILIGHT.

The scene for Fog (Plate 31), also known as *Les Petits Savoyards*, is the tradesmen's entrance to Silvy's house and studio. Two itinerant musicians from Savoy are ready to play their

hurdy-gurdies. Silvy placed the musicians against the iron railings, with their suggestion of exclusion, and in the chilling fog characteristic of a northern European metropolis. This feat was technically impossible without major manipulation. Possibly Silvy used more than one negative, as he did on other occasions. The boughs of the trees were surely added to the negative by hand.

Plate 32 is likely to be *Sun*, also exhibited as *Le Premier rayon*. Here Silvy gave a twist to the image of the crossing-sweeper familiar from 'Poor Jo' in *Bleak House*. An Indian man, with a well-worn brush leaning by his side, extends his palm for payment for clearing a path across a mud- and dung-strewn thoroughfare. The over-emphatic treatment of shadows suggests that this photograph represented *Sun*. As with the Savoyard musicians, there is an effect of displacement.

Twilight is also known as *Evening Star* (Plate 33). In his book *Photographers of Genius at the Getty*, Weston Naef has analysed the photograph:

Camille Silvy

Plate 32

Studies on Light: Sun,
1859
320 x 258mm

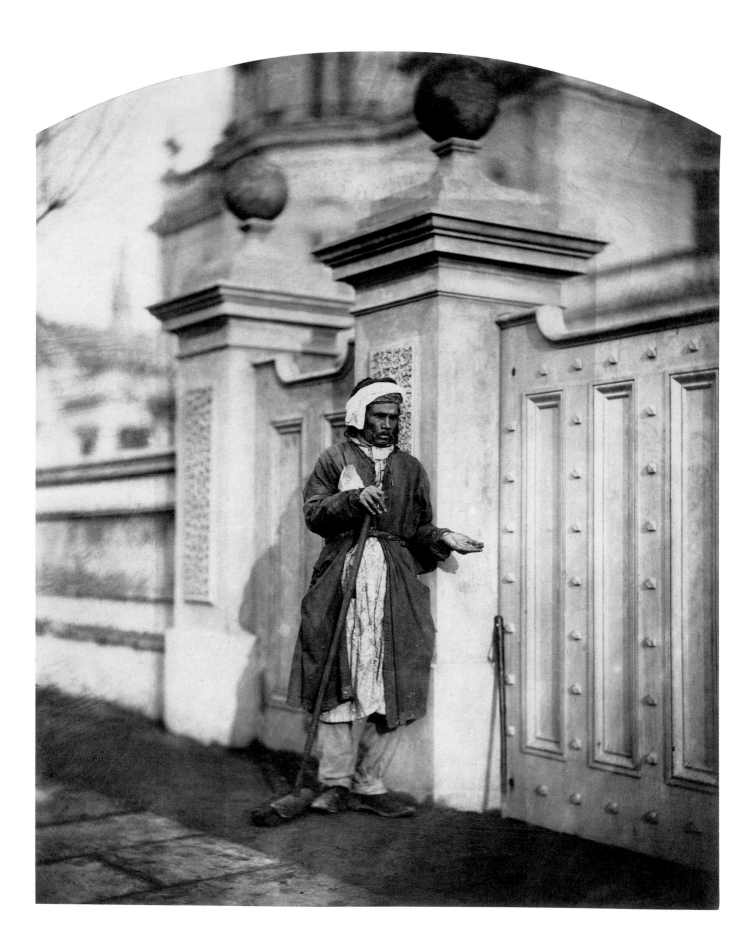

One negative was required for the street lamp, another for the foggy background, a third for the architecture at the right, and a fourth for the two standing figures. Clues to the artifice abound. We see moisture at the feet of the two figures reflecting light differently than do the surrounding surfaces. The join of one negative is along a line in the street to the right of the man, and the lump of black along the boy's back as it meets the lamp-post betrays the join of another negative.[13]

The light in the lamp may have been drawn on the negative as, unlike the lamps farther away, it has no aureole. The distant figure is probably the first intentional use of blur in the history of photography (see the detail shown in Plate 34). Here is the 'fugitive, fleeting beauty of present-day life', which Baudelaire placed at the heart of modernity.[14] Silvy's scene also conjures up the eerie world of Wilkie Collins (1824–89), author of *The Woman in White* (1860). The novel, serialised from November 1859, opens with a twilight walk to north London. Collins

lived as a boy at 30 Porchester Terrace – approximately where that uncanny blurred figure (male or female?) strolls or flees.

In a large still life, Silvy includes *The Times* newspaper for 11 November 1859 (Plate 35). At the back is a *papier peint* (printed wallpaper); in the centre a hare hangs beside a grouse, some coins, a knife, a pressed-glass bottle of salad dressing and *The Times*. Silvy updated a fine art convention to take account of new realities such as consumer goods and daily newspapers, which grew enormously in circulation and power during the 1850s. Silvy advertised regularly in *The Times* and other papers.[15] Silvy's 1859 *Still life* parallels a passage in *Le Déjeuner* (Luncheon in the Studio), 1868 by Édouard Manet (1832–83), in which linen, a lemon, oysters, blue and white porcelain and fine glass are joined by a lowly bottle of beer.

Plate 33

Studies on Light: Twilight, 1859
281 x 221mm

Plate 34

Detail of Plate 33

Plate 35

Still life, 1859
490 x 376mm

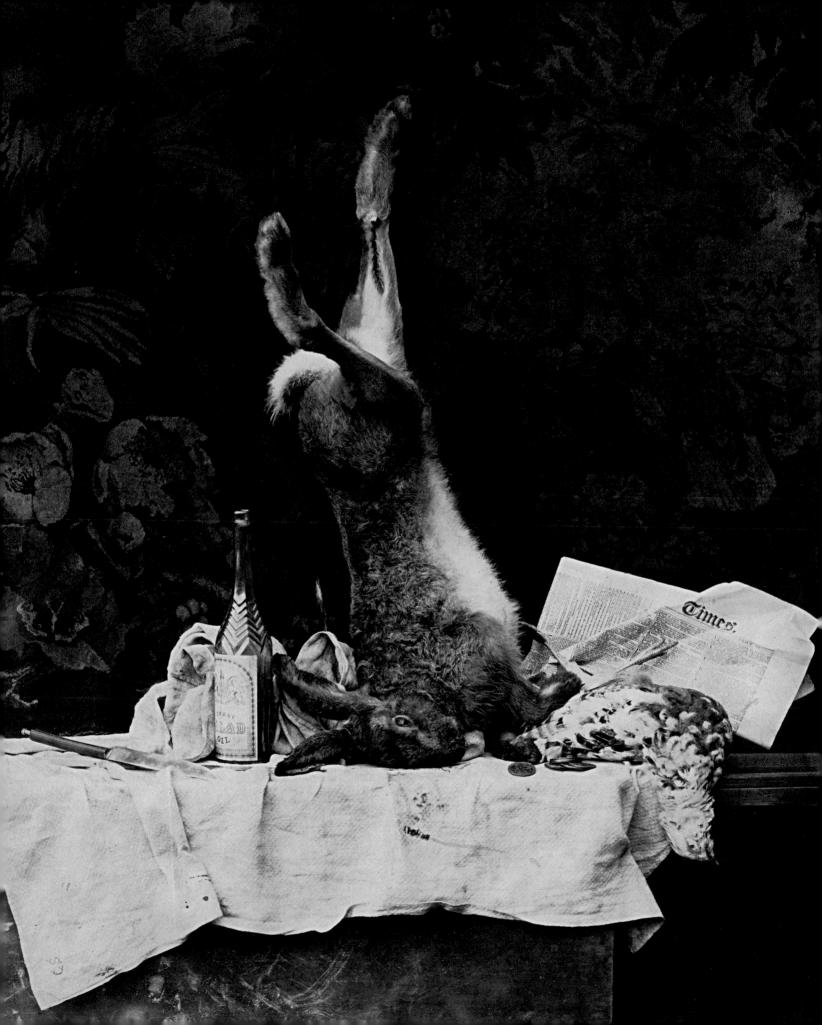

Chapter 4 | Camille Silvy and C. Silvy & Co.

Chapter 4 | Camille Silvy and C. Silvy & Co.

At the beginning of his London career Silvy had made around 200 portraits of actors and actresses, as Juliet Hacking brilliantly deduced in her doctoral thesis, and she rightly suggested that this enhanced his expressive repertoire.[1] The players needed promotional pictures and the photographer wanted an inventory to sell (Plate 36). Silvy wrote to his father on 6 June 1860 that he was impatient to enlarge his studio and construct workshops and laboratories in the backyard at Porchester Terrace. He had ordered six dozen printing frames but wrote that he also needed a printer. He had just sold 800 of his portraits of actors and actresses at a fundraising event for a new college of drama and had made a shilling from each portrait. It seems that Silvy's father doubted the profitability of cartes; however, his son retorted, 'these little bits of card have brought to the enterprise ['*l'oeuvre*'] around 7000 francs in one day.'

Silvy responded to the humour of his comic subjects (as can be seen in Plate 37). He photographed the 'Princess's Theatre Rifles', a corps de ballet in a production of Henry Byron's *Jack the Giant Killer*, in the winter of 1859–60 (Plate 38).[2] This pantomime patriotism was occasioned by the Volunteer Movement, which began in England in 1859 in response to fears of war with France. (Silvy joined the Artists' Rifles but was not called upon to fight the French.) The third and last issue of Silvy's *London Photographic Review* in the latter part of 1860 featured four photographs of the Hungarian opera singer Rosa Csillag (1832–92), who appeared in a production of Gluck's *Orfeo ed Euridice* at the Royal Italian Opera Covent Garden (as it was then known) on 27 June 1860 (Plate 39). The photographs were taken, it was noted on the title page, 'By Special Desire of Her Most Gracious Majesty the Queen'.[3]

The great coloratura soprano Adelina Patti (1843–1919) sat for Silvy on many occasions. His cartes of the singer sold in huge numbers – 20,000 copies according to a report in 1862.[4] To counteract piracy, Silvy copyrighted nineteen of his portraits of Patti between 1862 and 1867.[5] He photographed her

spectacularly: the dress was grand, the pose articulated, the background – a hunting scene – special to the sitting (Plate 40). To convey a sense of spontaneous action, Silvy added an attendant (stuffed) hound. Singer and photographer created an even greater sense of spontaneity with Patti's open mouth suggesting a live performance (Plate 41). Silvy also produced a large, sombre and powerful tableau entitled *Shylock and Jessica* (Plate 42).

Silvy put considerable effort into his fancy-dress costumes. He wore an elaborate outfit (shown in Plate 43) to a ball given in Paris on 12 March 1863 by the Pereire brothers – founders of Crédit Mobilier in 1852 and major financiers of the Second Empire. It was on that day that Silvy met Alice Monnier (1839–1912), who became his wife on 8 June the same year. Alice was from a prominent family in the Jura department, and the daughter of Alexandre Monnier (1814–81), an historian.

An untrimmed carte-de-visite shows Silvy in his pomp (Plate 44). Compared

to his earlier studio (as seen in Plate 17), this refurbished version of it is higher, deeper and grander. Silvy stands beside a plinth topped by *Cupids Fighting Over a Heart* (*c.*1780) by P.P. Thomire (1751–1843) and beyond is a landscape tapestry. On the right is Alice Silvy and beside her Mme Monnier, her aunt. Hand to head is Silvy's mother, then his young brother-in-law Marcel Monnier (who became an explorer and photographer) and on the left is Alexandre Monnier. As is usual in Silvy's portraits, the sitters were encouraged – not entirely successfully in this case – to look to the side of the camera. A cradle suggests that the family had gathered in London for the impending birth of Louise-Marie-Elisabeth-Angèle Silvy in 1866. Born on Easter Day ('Pâques'), she was nicknamed 'Pâquerette'. Silvy's son, Jean-Marie-Léon-Lazare-Enée, was born in 1868.

One of Silvy's most important associates was the sculptor Baron Carlo Marochetti (1805–67) (Plate 45). Carlo Marochetti was close to Prince Albert and made important public statues, including *Richard the Lionheart* (1860), seen here

Plate 37

Two portraits of Frederick Robson, 1859–60
Left: 86 x 58mm
Right: 86 x 58mm

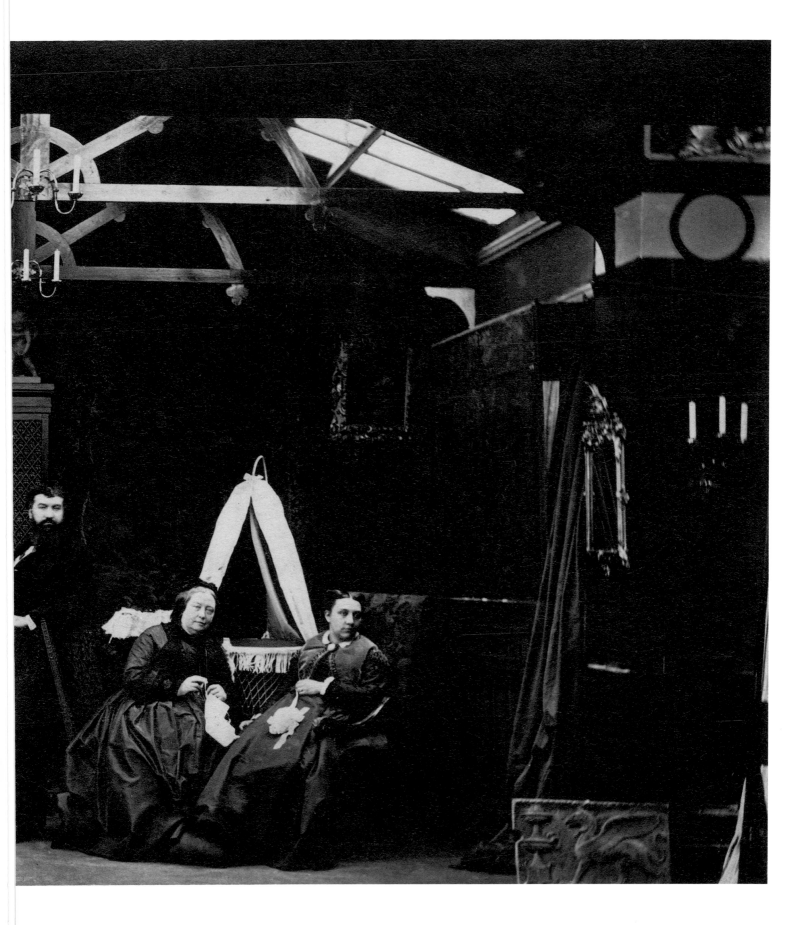

Chapter 5 | A closer look at cartes

Chapter 5 | A closer look at cartes

Wedding photography began in the early 1850s, but Silvy may have been the first to use the carte-de-visite format for the genre (Plate 52). Constantia Nicolaides, cataloguer of the Daybooks at the National Portrait Gallery, has established that the subject of this photograph, Marion Clifford (*c*.1841–1919, née Morgan-Clifford), was associated with the royal household. The fashion historian Miles Lambert noted that 'Miss Morgan's veil is held in place by a wreath of orange blossom, the universal accompaniment to mid-Victorian white weddings. Orange blossom, associated with fertility, first appeared in England during the 1820s and quickly became popular, perhaps as a counterbalance to the virginal attributes of the veil.'[1] The portrait was taken in a private house and the relatively uncontrolled lighting burned out the detail in the dress and allowed little facial modelling. Thereafter Silvy's wedding photographs were taken in the studio, although he remained equipped to work on location. His mobile darkroom is seen in a suite of photographs made at Orléans House, Twickenham in June 1864 (Plate 53).

The occasion was a '*fête champêtre*' to raise funds for the Société Française de Bienfaisance in London. A 'Photographic Saloon' is seen beside his mobile darkroom. Silvy probably sold his photographs in a marquee that appears to have been set aside for the sale of art works.[2]

Silvy persuaded the authorities at the Palace of Westminster to allow him to set up a darkroom there so that he could photograph members of both Houses of Parliament (Plate 54). On 4 September 1860 he wrote to his father that he would be beginning a new line the following month – painted photographs: 'Thanks to the extreme finesse of my figures, the tints can be lightly applied without altering the photograph, producing in this way ravishing miniatures' (Plate 55). Silvy also teamed up with the Parisian inventor, Lafon de Camarsac (1821–1905), whose workshop created versions of Silvy's portraits in photo-enamel.[3]

Silvy was commissioned to make portraits of Prince Albert, Edward, Prince of Wales (1841–1910), and

Princess Alice (1843–78) in 1861. Silvy kept a *'Livre d'Or'* – an album of autographed royal portraits (Plate 56). Silvy's portrait of Princess Alice embellished the cover (at the lower right) of a luxurious carte-de-visite album (as seen in Plate 57). Albums soon became available at all levels of complexity and cost, sometimes with elegant arches in gold ink. Silvy used mirrors to include face and coiffure (Plate 58). Such albums became a feature of the parlours of Victorian England, the focus of a social ritual involving families and imagined communities.[4] Silvy captured the absorbed psychological state of looking at and sharing such albums (Plate 59).

Other important commissions deriving from the royal household included portraits of Mr and Mrs J.P.L. Davies (Plates 60 and 61). Mrs Davies was known before her marriage as Sarah Forbes Bonetta (*c.*1842–80). In 1850, as a child of about eight, she had been given to the captain of the warship *Bonetta* by the ruler of Dahomey (Benin). The captain could not refuse the gift because the girl, the captive

daughter of a chief, would otherwise have been killed. Queen Victoria became the child's godmother and undertook her education. Bonetta was described as 'a perfect genius' who picked up English quickly and had a special talent for music.[5] She married J.P.L. Davies, a Lagos merchant, on 14 August 1862. It is likely that the Queen not only suggested but also paid for the portrait sitting: the royal accounts show a payment of £3 for cartes of Mrs Davies. Silvy also made larger – more expensive – portraits of the newly-weds (as shown in Plate 61). Photographs of this size, usually found only in the albums of the very affluent, give an even more vivid image of this impressive couple.

The Dowager Queen Emma of the Sandwich Islands (now Hawaii), on a visit to England to meet missionary groups, sat for Silvy in 1865 (Plate 62). Queen Emma (1836–85), the daughter of a Hawaiian high chief and an English woman, married King Kamehameha IV in 1856. After he died in 1863, Queen Emma was photographed in full mourning dress. William Ellis, an English missionary and pioneering

Plate 52

Marion Clifford (née Morgan-Clifford), Lady Dunboyne, 1860
85 x 53mm

Plate 53

Untitled, from the album
*Orléans House Fête
Champêtre, Juin 1864,*
1864
100 x 175mm

Plate 54

Lord George Henry
Cavendish, Samuel
Gregson and Edward
Gordon Douglas-Pennant,
1st Baron Penrhyn at the
Palace of Westminster,
1860
86 x 57mm

Plate 55

Hand-painted miniature
portrait in plush-lined
case, 1860–7
44 x 36mm

photographer, described her as 'a young, intelligent, and well-educated lady of highest rank'.[6]

Silvy was well known for more elaborate, personalised settings (like the ones shown in Plate 63). A painter, a geologist, a bishop and two Orléans princes were provided with appropriate accessories and backcloths. Silvy had many backcloths, which were painted on both sides (thirty backcloths were listed in the 1869 auction catalogue). Portraits were individualised in many ways. Monsieur Gaugiran was posed beside a table overflowing with papers – one has the title *Vie des Champs* so perhaps he was a journalist of hunting or of the turf (Plate 64). Captain Frederick Robertson Aikman VC (1828–88) is richly self-coded: his bravery at the battle of Goomtee River in 1858, where he received a sabre slash to the face, was recognised by the award of the Victoria Cross (Plate 65). Gillian Brewer of the National Army Museum elucidates:

Aikman is wearing the uniform of the 3rd Sikh Cavalry (disbanded in 1861): a dark blue 'kurtah' (a long blouse or frock fastened from the neck to the waist); a 'kummerband' or long silk sash, tied around the waist. The lace trim around the cuff and neck would have been silver. Aikman is holding a forage cap; officers wore this type of cap whilst off duty. Over his left shoulder is his 'pouch belt' made of silver thread, with ornamental silver 'pickers', on chains. (Originally these pointed pieces of metal were used to clean out the touch-hole of a pistol or carbine.) A sword belt is worn around the waist over the kummerband; hanging from this is a sword and a sabretache. The early hussars wore tight breeches, which did not permit pockets and so their purse or pouch was worn on the waistbelt. The sabretache is decorated with the cypher of the 3rd Sikh Cavalry.[7]

In Plate 66 the Honourable Reverend William Charles Ellis stands proudly beside what appears to be an invention of his own. Scientists posed with vessels possibly furnished from Silvy's laboratory (Plate 67) Many sitters posed with a photograph from Silvy's portfolio (Plate 68). Theodore Fawcett (1832–98)

settled in Western Australia in 1859 and became a farmer, Justice of the Peace, brandy distiller and politician. Silvy's portraits show Fawcett in contrasting guises – man of learning and of the bush (Plates 69 and 70). Silvy also tried out the postage stamp portrait, using his father-in-law to demonstrate it (Plate 71). However, Silvy's greatest achievement in portraiture was an apparently simple one but actually quite rare at the time: he presented modern people as themselves (Plate 72 is a fine example of this).

A page from the Daybooks of 1862 shows a copy of a painted miniature of a soldier; two portraits of a dead baby; a copy of a daguerreotype of Balzac (Plate 73). The post-mortems are captioned 'Reproduction' but may be by Silvy himself. Even in this sad branch of the art, photographers would arrange the subject: one hand clasps a cross, the other poignantly reaches out.[8] The daguerreotype portrait of Honoré de Balzac (1799–1850), known as *Balzac à la bretelle* (Balzac in braces) was taken by Louis-Auguste Bisson in 1842. According to Nadar's memoir,

Silvy acquired the portrait from the Parisian caricaturist Paul Gavarni (1804–66). Silvy surely knew the story related by Nadar about Balzac's fear of photography. According to him 'all physical bodies are made up entirely of ghost-like images' and one of these 'leaf-like layers' was thought to be removed each time a photograph was taken.[9] Daguerreotypes were unique items, whereas Silvy's portraits were produced on an industrial scale. Balzac, for all his immense productivity, was a one-man band. His successors in the 1850s, such as Alexandre Dumas (1802–70), ran novel factories using teams of writers.[10] C. Silvy & Co. was also a factory, as was apparent when Prince Albert died suddenly in December 1861. There was an enormous demand for his portrait and Silvy's studio probably provided many of the estimated 70,000 ordered from Marion & Co. in the week following the Consort's death.[11] The studio made a new carte, an oval bust-length enlargement from the portrait taken earlier that year. The Daybooks have four copies of the posthumous portrait – meaning that there were at least four glass negatives (each with six

Plate 56

Prince Albert in Silvy's *Livre d'Or* (visitors' book) of autographed royal portraits – with Albert's autograph below, 1861 85 x 57mm

93

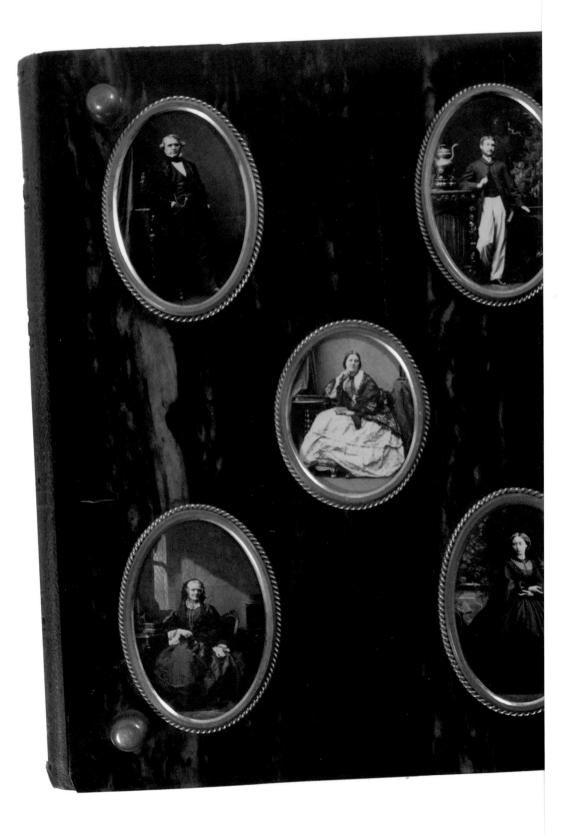

Plate 59

The children of Mrs
Ricardo (Miss Ricardo;
Master Ricardo), 1860
82 x 56mm

Plate 60

Sarah Forbes Bonetta
(Sarah Davies), 1862
83 x 56mm

Plate 61

James Pinson Labulo
Davies and Sarah Forbes
Bonetta (Sarah Davies),
1862
108 x 129mm

Plate 71

Proof sheet of postage
stamp portrait of
Alexandre Monnier,
*c.*1866 (detail)
145 x 222mm

Plate 72

J. Gialussi, 1861
84 x 55mm

Plate 73

A page from Daybook
Vol.7: copy of a miniature
of a soldier; two post-
mortem photographs;
and a daguerreotype of
Honoré de Balzac (1842),
1862
Album page: 308 x 244mm

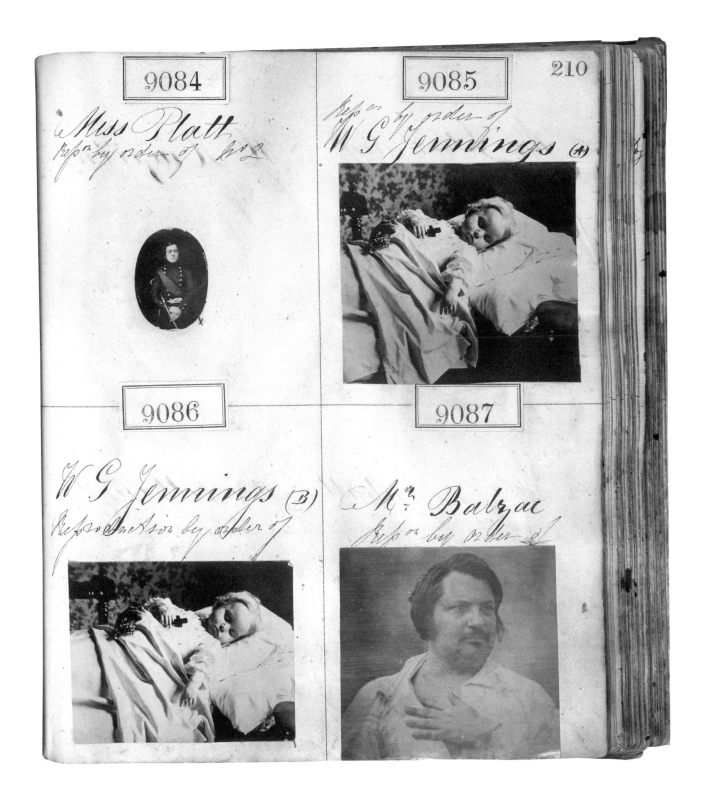

9084

Miss Platt
Repr by order of his

9085

Repr by order of
W G Jennings (A)

9086

W G Jennings (B)
Reproduction by order of

9087

Mr Balzac
Repr by order of

Chapter 6 | Mode to modernity

Chapter 6 | Mode to modernity

Plate 76

Mrs Holford's daughter.
1860
85 x 56mm

Page 114
The Misses Booth, 1861
(detail)
see Plate 84

Baudelaire argued that 'The idea of beauty which man creates for himself imprints itself on his whole attire, crumples or stiffens the dress, rounds off or squares his gesture, and in the long run even ends by subtly penetrating the very features of his face.'[1] He observed that a woman and her dress, usually thought of as separate, actually form 'an indivisible unity'.[2] Silvy's cartes, in keeping with the poet's insights, are often fashion-portraits.

Silvy's photographs of young children also involve fashionable dress. Without the Daybook captions it would be impossible to distinguish girls from boys as boys wore dresses until 'breeched' around the age of four (Plates 76–8). Silvy lavished attention on his young sitters, from the most delicate lighting to wondrous accessories. He allowed infants to choose poses that seem at once completely unconventional and entirely natural (Plate 79). Servants sometimes took charge of children or babies during a sitting. Thus, there is the portrait of an Indian servant with Mrs Herbert Davis' children (Plate 80), several nursemaids (including the one in Plate 81), and

'Miss Gough's governess', a soberly dressed young woman in a dress of plain silk or wool and a crinoline of modest size, posing with minimal self-display (Plate 82). The visibility of the Misses Marjoribanks' ankles (Plate 83) suggests that they were still pre-teen. The younger sister seems to be speaking to her older sibling as she gazes at an album. Silvy used a different trick to animate another of his double portraits (Plate 84). He created a tableau in which the young women lightly clasp hands and form, with the help of an adroitly placed Venetian mirror, an intimate triangle of heads. Silvy's portrait of Miss Callander (Plate 85) reminds us that the crinoline was not an encumbrance. It did away with the multiple petticoats which rendered women relatively immobile. As the fashion historian Valerie Steele remarks: 'The swinging of the crinoline imparted a new, flirtatious aspect to women's dress …'.[3] It was shown in action as part of walking costume (Plate 86). There were many inventive collaborations between photographer and client. A mother is seen only from the back, perhaps to focus attention on the

Plate 77

Arthur Lewin Enthoven,
1861
84 x 56mm

118

Plate 78
Miss Anderson, 1861
85 x 56mm

Camille Silvy

Plate 79

Master Surtees, 1862
96 x 64mm

Plate 80

Mrs Herbert Davis'
children and servant,
1866
82 x 56mm

121

Plate 81

Mrs Gregory's babe and
nurse, 1865
83 x 57mm

brightly lit child (Plate 87). Because of
his almost cinematic control of lighting,
Silvy could depict children as hauntingly
as Dickens (Plate 88).

Silvy's great contribution surely lay
in the thousands of portraits he made
that are not overtly original but simply
authentic. The daughter of Lady Stanley
of Alderley takes the natural stance, so
to speak, of a woman of standing in mid-
Victorian England (Plate 89). Another
of the specialities of Silvy and his clients
was the portrait of reflection, of someone
absorbed in their own thoughts (as
shown in Plate 90). One of the reasons
for the vivid expressions and natural
deportment of Silvy's fashion portraits is
their size. A contemporary noted: 'The
question of expression is less a problem
in album portraits than in larger
pictures. In many cases the rapidity with
which they are taken renders natural
expression easy …'.[4]

Silvy made larger portraits when
commissioned, such as the portrait of
Mrs Cartledge in mourning dress (Plate
91). The larger negative brings with it
a more exact – and exquisite – rendering
of face, figure and costume, but also
an undeniable formality of posture.
Silvy shows us the women of the haute
bourgeoisie who dressed 'not to attract
rich patrons but rather for an active
social life. Their role – at soirées, balls,
receptions, the races, the theatre, etc. –
was to look beautiful and elegant.'[5] That
kind of public elegance is exemplified
by Silvy's portrait of Robert and
Françoise d'Orléans, duc and duchesse
de Chartres (Plate 92). The portrait
was taken soon after Robert d'Orléans
(1840–1910) had returned to England
after fighting on the Union side in the
American Civil War.

In the portrait of Miss James (Plate 93),
the pointed-back chair that had seated
so many ecclesiastics now sets the scene
for a Gothic novel. Her hair was dressed
in a new 'tangled' style, which Anthony
Trollope (1815–82) noted in his character
Miss Madalina Demolines, in *The Last
Chronicle of Barset* (serialised in 1866–7).
In the same novel, Trollope referred to
a bourgeois drawing room at an address
in Porchester Terrace, which contained a
'photograph book' for the entertainment
of visitors. This was surely an album

Plate 82

Miss Gough's governess,
1865
84 x 56mm

of cartes, suggesting that the format —
if no longer a craze — was still
fashionable.[6] Coincidentally, one of the
novel's most dramatic scenes involves
a policeman with his 'bull's-eye' lantern
on the pavement in Porchester Terrace.[7]
Silvy had used the same street as the
setting for his photograph of *Twilight*
in the autumn of 1859 (Plate 33). In the
portrait of Miss James, the studio light,
which had suggested so many summer
days in a rococo pleasaunce, was boldly
transformed into moonlight. Silvy and
Madame Labalmondière created an
outdoor moonlit tableau (Plate 94).
The carte of Miss Valpy (Plate 95),
probably from May 1867, is quite
possibly one of Silvy's last.[8] Miss Valpy,
a modern young woman in walking
clothes, is about to set off into the city.
The history of fashion photography
began with pictures like this.

Chapter 7 | 1867 and after

Detail of Plate 97
360 degree panorama of
Champs Elysées from the
Rond Point, 1867

his memoir, Silvy showed more serious symptoms. The celebrated Dr Emile Blanche (1820–93), who treated Gérard de Nerval (1808–55) and later Guy de Maupassant (1850–93), diagnosed '*folie raisonnante*', a delusional form of psychosis.[9] The alternation of periods of high creativity and depression – with periods of lucidity – would in later terminology suggest a diagnosis of manic depression and in today's parlance bipolar disorder. He was cared for in La Croix-du-Perche by his mother. After her death in 1874, Silvy's condition worsened severely and his crises became violent. From 1876 Silvy spent a year and a half at the 'Pensionnat' in Ville-Evrard (near Paris) and after his discharge returned to Nogent. He was jailed after a fracas in July 1878. Dr Hamel, a local doctor who knew Silvy well, was commissioned by the *préfet* to examine him in prison. Following Dr Hamel's report, Silvy was committed to psychiatric asylums for the last thirty-one years of his life.[10] He died from bronchopneumonia in the Hôpital de St Maurice (Charenton) on 2 February 1910. If he had been born a century later, perhaps some milligrams of salts of lithium would have transformed his life.

One of the most surprising pages of the Daybooks offers two contrasting Silvy self-portraits (Plates 98 and 99). On the left we see Silvy wearing an elegant suit, an artistic smoking hat, flowing tie and dapper side-whiskers pointed and waxed in the style of the Emperor himself. This is Silvy the former and future diplomat, Silvy the studio proprietor and public benefactor. On the right Silvy wears something halfway between a hairnet and a skullcap, an open-necked striped shirt with a loosely knotted cravat and an unbuttoned jacket. This Silvy is closer to the camera, larger and more intimately seen as he lounges against a piece of furniture. The background is indeterminate and out of focus. The face is shown more obliquely and has a downward tilt. Is this Silvy the unkempt artist, brother to the unbuttoned, inspired, exhausted Balzac in the daguerreotype he owned? Is this the pair of Silvys that Camille referred to in a letter to his father at the beginning of his London career – Silvy, the artist, versus C. Silvy & Co., a business? Was this the creative tension that eventually snapped?

Plate 100

Spring, *c.*1860
270 x 203mm

In 1868 Silvy had printed an *Alphabet de Pâquerette, Composé et photographié par C. Silvy, Londres 1868* for his daughter's second birthday. His neatly rhyming quatrains refer to a number of items we find in one of Silvy's most delightful photographs (Plate 100). Perhaps this photograph was intended to accompany the poem. If not, it is a poetic equivalent to the text and shows that Silvy was capable of creating a large tableau celebrating not only childhood (another theme recommended by Baudelaire to his modern painter), but also the light of springtime and joy. It is most likely to be a photograph titled *Spring* from early in Silvy's London career.[11]

In 1869 Silvy published an *Ode à la Reine de la Paix et de l'Abondance.* He wrote of arriving as an unknown in the vast metropolis of London – perhaps this explains the empathy with immigrants shown in his street photographs. He gallantly – but also truthfully – attributed his success to the benign influence of Queen Victoria. He described photography, the art he cultivated, as 'rapidly taking things in', but incapable of equalling creative art –

'L'Art que je cultivais, rapide observateur, / Ne peut marcher de pair avec l'Art créateur'. He wrote that 'the artist and the poet unite and their work transmits to posterity the feeling [or sensation] that the heart dictated' – *'l'artiste et le poète / S'unissent, et leur œuvre à la posterité / Transmet le sentiment que le cœur a dicté'*. He sought only a modest place for his photographic achievements as a helper to the fine arts, 'showing you details and new effects' – *'Vous montrant des détails et des effets nouveaux'*. Surely no photographer ever made a more modest self-assessment. However, Nadar – his great contemporary, who knew him so well – put it this way: 'This photographer and his studio … had no equals.'[12]

Acknowledgements

My warmest thanks to Camille Silvy's descendants in Paris for their generous help and great kindness over many years, in particular to Françoise Monnier-Dominjon. My gratitude is also due in full measure to the staff of the Département des Estampes et de la photographie at the Bibliothèque nationale de France, Paris; the Department of Photographs, the Getty Research Institute and the Scholars and Seminar Program at the J. Paul Getty Museum, Los Angeles; the Photography Department (especially Clare Freestone, Constantia Nicolaides and Terence Pepper) and the Heinz Archive at the National Portrait Gallery, London; the Theatre Collection and the Department of Word & Image at the Victoria and Albert Museum, London. I am greatly indebted to many friends and colleagues, including those whose names appear in the bibliography, and also to Dr Natalie Adamson (University of St Andrews), Sylvie Aubenas (Bibliothèque nationale de France), Gordon Baldwin, Gillian Brewer (National Army Museum), Marie-Sophie Corcy (Musée des arts et métiers), Simon Franses, Peter Galassi (The Museum of Modern Art), Philippe Garner, Peter Hamilton, Violet Hamilton (Wilson Photography Centre), Professor John Hannavy, Colin Harding (National Media Museum), Ken and Jenny Jacobson, Liz Jobey, Patrick Kinmonth, Anne Lacoste and Paul Martineau (J. Paul Getty Museum), Jennifer Lister (Textiles & Fashion, V&A), Caroline Marten, Sarah McDonald (Getty Images), Anne de Mondenard, Steve Moriarty (Snite Museum, University of Notre Dame), Aaron Olivas – my research assistant at the Getty in 2008 (UCLA), Alistair O'Neill, Erin O'Toole (San Francisco Museum of Modern Art), Marc Pagneux, Michael Pritchard (webmaster, British Photographic History), Françoise Reynaud (Musée Carnavalet), Michael S. Sachs, Marcel Safier, Dietmar Siegert, Professor Paul Smith, Tessa Traeger, Carole Troufléau (Société française de photographie) and Colin Westerbeck.

Picture credits

Index